MAKE it WORK!

PHOTOGRAPHY

Andrew Haslam & Jon Barnes

written by
Kathryn Senior

Photography: Jon Barnes
Consultant: Graham Peacock
Senior Lecturer in Science Education at
Sheffield Hallam University

TWO-CAN
in association with
WATTS BOOKS

MAKE it WORK!
Other titles

Body
Building
Earth
Electricity
Flight
Insects
Machines
Plants
Sound
Space
Time

First published in Great Britain in 1996 by
Two-Can Publishing Ltd
346 Old Street
London EC1V 9NQ
in association with
Watts Books
96 Leonard Street
London EC2A 4RH

Printed in Hong Kong

Hardback 2 4 6 8 10 9 7 5 3 1
Paperback 2 4 6 8 10 9 7 5 3 1

Dewey Decimal Classification: 915.4

A catalogue record for this book is available from the British Library.

Hardback ISBN: 1 85434 360 2
Paperback ISBN: 1 85434 362 9

Editor: Robert Sved
Designer: Helen McDonagh
Project Editor: Kate Graham
Managing Editor: Christine Morley
Managing Art Director: Carole Orbell
Production: Joya Bart-Plange
Series concept and design: Andrew Haslam and Wendy Baker
Additional photography: Ray Moller

Thanks also to: Katharine and Jonathan Bee, Sarah Martinez, James Davis,
Jamie Bignal, Thanujah Yogarajah, Ivan Lau, Louise Chan, Marisa Hawthorn
and everyone at Plough Studios.

Contents

Words marked in **bold** in the text are explained in the glossary.

Photography allows you to be a scientist and an artist at the same time. Most people take photographs to record events but, by experimenting with a camera and making your own **prints**, you can create all sorts of different effects.

You will need

You can make the models in this book using simple materials such as balsa wood, card, tape and paper. For some projects, you will need to use small **lenses** which you can buy from model shops. Some materials are special to photography. Photographic solutions, photographic film and paper, film canisters and film spools are all available from specialist shops or large stores with photographic departments.

hacksaw

spanner

screwdriver

pencil

scissors

drill

ruler

vice

glue gun

bradawl

clamp

Photographers work in many areas: medicine and astronomy, as well as fashion, sport, news reporting and in books and magazines.

MAKE it WORK!

Building the models in this book will show you some of the basic techniques needed to take photographs. You will see how light makes images on photographic paper and film, how different cameras work, and how you can develop and process your own photographs.

Cutting, drilling and joining

You will need some tools to cut the materials. Measure each part accurately, marking with a pencil before cutting things out and drilling holes. Always cut away from your fingers. When you have cut wood, sand off any sharp edges with sandpaper. When you need to drill a hole, use a pointed bradawl to start the hole and then finish it off with a hand drill. A glue gun is useful for joining parts of models.

Safety!

Sharp tools are dangerous! Always take care and ask an adult to help you. Make sure that anything you drill is held firmly so that it does not slip. A small table vice is ideal for holding wood. Always use rubber gloves and tongs when using photographic solutions.

watch

torch

Setting up a dark room

Photographic paper is coated with chemicals that change when ordinary light falls on the paper, so you need to handle your paper in a dark room with a red safety light. A small room with a sink makes an ideal dark room. Cover windows with black dustbin bags or black paper. Light the room with a torch covered in a red plastic **gel** or a lamp with a red light bulb. Fumes from photographic chemicals must not be breathed in for long periods of time, so have a break outside the room every 15 minutes.

Buying photographic paper and film

This book will help you decide what you need to use to make your prints. There are many types of paper and film to choose from, so make sure you know what kind of photographs you will be taking before you buy your equipment.

timer

contact frame

Making prints

To make your own photographs you will have to buy solutions from a specialist shop. There are many different brands and you will need to **dilute** most of them before use. Follow the manufacturer's dilution and temperature instructions carefully.

torch with red gel

thermometer

rubber gloves

fixer

photographic paper

measuring cylinder

tray   funnel   tongs

photographic film and canisters

developer

Light is a type of **energy** produced by the Sun, electric light bulbs and candles. In photography, light **reflected** from an object enters a camera through the lens. Where light hits the chemicals on the surface of photographic paper or film, an **image** is formed.

MAKE it WORK!
You can make a ray box and use it to investigate light.

You will need
glue	a craft knife
lenses	a small mirror
a prism	a glass of water
scissors	thin balsa-wood strips
a battery	two paperclips and wires
thin card	a small bulb and bulb holder

1 Cut out the card as shown above. The square flaps should measure 10 cm x 10 cm. With an adult's help, cut out the window using a craft knife. Score along the dotted lines.

2 To make the grill, glue the balsa-wood strips over the window, as shown below left.

3 Fold the card to form a box. The balsa-wood strips should be inside the box. Glue the flaps together using the tabs.

Using your ray box
Connect the bulb to the paperclips with two wires. Now attach one paperclip to each battery terminal. Make the room dark and place the ray box over the bulb. You will see light spreading out in the shape of a fan. Notice that each light beam is a straight line. Light always travels in straight lines.

For these experiments, you will need to block off most of your grill. Fix two pieces of black card inside your box with tape so that light can only pass through a small section of the grill. You will now see one or two beams of light.

▲ Reflection

Look at the effect of shining a single beam of light into a mirror. Mirrors are very good reflectors of light. You should see that all the light that reaches the mirror is reflected back. Try changing the angle of the mirror and see what happens.

▲ Splitting white light

Light looks white, but really it is made up of many colours. Shine a light beam through a prism and you will see that white light splits into red, orange, yellow, green, blue, indigo and violet light.

▼ Bending light

Light can pass through objects that are **transparent**, but not through objects that are **opaque**. Some transparent objects can cause a beam of light to **refract**. Shine a light beam through a glass of water. You can see that it does not travel straight through: the refracted beam is at an angle to the original.

◄ Using lenses

If you pass light beams through a **convex lens**, the beams **focus** at a single point. The distance between the lens and this point is the focal length of the lens. As light travels in straight lines, the beams continue in their new direction travelling away from each other. What happens when you shine light through a **concave lens**?

You will need

two strips of thick balsa wood, 25 cm x 2 cm
a small lens in a round plastic holder
a piece of glass, 25 cm x 25 cm

a candle	a pencil
Plasticine	thin and thick tape
thick card	a mirror, 25 cm x 35 cm
tracing paper	scissors and a craft knife

1 Cut the card into the same shape as you did for the box on page 6. Each square flap should measure 25 cm x 25 cm.

2 With an adult's help, use a craft knife to cut a circle the same size as the lens holder in the centre of the top flap. Score the card as before. Glue the flaps together using the tabs.

3 Put the mirror into the box, so that it lies diagonally across the box with the mirrored side facing the hole. In this picture, you can see the hole in the top reflected in the mirror.

4 Glue two balsa-wood strips to the sides of the open end.

The term 'camera obscura' is Latin for 'darkened chamber'. In a camera obscura, light enters through a lens in one side. It is then reflected by a mirror forming an image on the screen at the top of the camera. There the image can be traced onto paper easily. These first cameras were used by artists for sketching views.

MAKE it WORK!
Use your own camera obscura to produce and trace an image of a candle.

5 Tape tracing paper to one side of the glass and place the glass, paper face down, on top of the wood strips. Tape it in place with thick tape. Squeeze the lens into the hole.

Experiments with your camera obscura

You will need to find a room with hard flooring. It is best to tape a piece of silver foil onto the floor to protect it from hot wax. Use Plasticine to hold your candle securely in place.

Carefully light the candle and put the camera a short distance away. Use some dark material to cover your head and the camera, so that you can look at the screen at the top of the camera. Keep the material well away from the candle. You may need to move your camera backwards and forwards, but you should be able to see a clear image of the candle on the screen.

Remember! Never leave a lit candle unattended.

Drawing the image

Tape another piece of tracing paper or some thin drawing paper over the screen. Now use a pencil to trace the image of the candle. Try using your camera obscura to draw other objects.

The camera obscura was first used in China in the seventh century. Alhazen, a 10th-century Arabian philosopher, used one to look at the Sun. The camera obscura was first described in detail in the 15th century by Leonardo da Vinci.

If you removed the mirror from the camera obscura, the image would appear, upside down, at the back of the camera. In a modern camera, photographic film lies across the back of the camera to record the image.

MAKE it WORK!

You can use a room that has only one small window to make a giant camera. If you move the position of the image in the giant camera you will see why modern cameras have their film fixed in one position. The following experiment works best on a sunny day.

You will need

an artist's easel or a chair with a piece of board
large sheets of black paper
pens and pencils   tape
white paper   a pin

1 Ask an adult to help you black out the window using black paper and tape. Use a pin to make a tiny hole in the centre of the paper.

2 Set up the easel in the middle of the room. Tape some white paper onto the easel.

3 Make sure the room light is off. You may have to move the easel backwards and forwards to get a clear image.

Looking at the image

The wall opposite your window should be filled with a giant, upside down, or **inverted**, image of what is outside your window. A small part of the image should appear on the paper on your easel. Try moving your easel nearer and further away from the window until the image on the paper is as clear as you can get it.

Change the angle of the board so that the left edge is nearer the window than the right. Draw the image that you see. Now do the same with the bottom edge nearer the window. How are these images different from the image made when the board is directly facing the window?

▶ If you move your paper down so that it lies almost flat, the image will get longer and become very distorted.

▲ To see your image in proportion, the paper must be directly facing the window.

▲ If the paper is kept upright but turned slightly to the left or right, your image will look wider.

Camera images

In a modern camera, photographic film sits inside the back of the camera so that it directly faces the lens. If the back of the camera is not flat, the image on the film will be distorted like the pictures of the tree shown above.

Why is the image inverted?

Light travels in straight lines. Some of the light that is reflected off the top of the object passes through the pinhole to the bottom of the wall. Some of the light from the bottom of the object passes through the pinhole to the top of the wall. In this way, light beams from all over the object travel through the pinhole in straight lines, forming an inverted image on the wall.

When light beams from an object enter your eye, they are focused by a lens onto the back of the eye forming an upside down image. So our eyes 'see' everything upside down and it is our brain that turns the image the right way up.

12 Pinhole Cameras

The pinhole camera is the simplest camera you can use to take photographs. Light enters through a pinhole at one end of the camera and falls onto a piece of photographic paper at the other. When the paper is **developed**, an inverted **negative** image can be seen.

1 Cut the card into the two shapes shown below. For your black base box, each square flap should measure 10 cm. You will need to make your yellow top box 1 mm bigger all round, so that it fits over the base box.

2 With an adult's help, use a craft knife to cut a 2 cm diameter circle in the centre of the bottom flap of the yellow card. Make a pinhole in the centre of the corresponding flap in the black card.

MAKE it WORK!

You can make a pinhole camera and use it to take your own pictures using photographic paper. To load and unload your camera you will need to use a dark room.

You will need

two thin strips of balsa wood	glue
thick black and yellow card	tape
photographic paper	a pin
a craft knife	scissors

3 Score along the dotted lines and glue your boxes together using the tabs.

4 For the photographic paper holder, cut a piece of black card with tabs and a central window, as shown above. The dotted lines form a 10 cm square and the window is 8 cm square. Place a piece of card, 10 cm square, on top of the window. Fold the flaps up and tape them to the back of the square card.

5 Place the paper holder in the back of the base box. The window must face the pinhole. Glue two balsa-wood strips inside the base box so that the paper holder will not fall forwards.

camera

paper holder

Finding something to photograph

Before you load your pinhole camera with photographic paper, you will need to find an object or scene to photograph. Try and find a bright scene that doesn't move. It is best to go outside or sit your camera on a window ledge on a sunny day. You can also take pictures indoors by placing objects next to a window or by using lamps to light your scene. A scene with a strong **contrast** will produce a better print so try and light your objects brightly so that they produce shadows.

On pages 14-15 you will see how to load your camera and take pictures.

Look at pages 30-31 to see how to use a lamp and some card to direct your lighting.

MAKE it WORK!

You are now ready to load your camera with photographic paper. Make sure that no ordinary light can enter your dark room and light the room with your safety light. You should try to touch the shiny side of the paper as little as possible.

You will need

a pinhole camera
photographic paper
a black light-tight box
scissors
safety light
a dark room

Photographic paper

Photographic paper is a thick paper coated with light-sensitive chemicals called emulsion. The shiny side is the emulsion side. When light falls on the emulsion, the chemicals change to record an image.

Once you have **exposed** the photographic paper, you need to store it in a light-tight box. This keeps it from being spoiled until you develop the print. Make a box from black card or paint a ready-made box black.

1 With your safety light on, take a piece of photographic paper from its box.

2 Using scissors, cut the paper so that it will fit into the paper holder.

3 Slide the paper, emulsion side towards you, into the paper holder. Touch the emulsion as little as possible.

4 Slide the paper holder back into position at the back of the camera so that the paper is facing the pinhole.

5 Put the lid back on your camera so that it rests about 2 cm from the base, covering the pinhole.

*Light-sensitive paper was invented by William Fox Talbot in 1839. With one exposure, the paper produced a negative image from which many **positive** prints could be made. A friend of Talbot's called the invention "photography".*

You will find that some of your pictures are very pale images with little contrast. These have been **under-exposed**. Others may be very dark. These have been **over-exposed**. Make a note of the time needed for the best exposure.

Taking photographs

Now it's time to take some pictures. Put your camera in position in front of your scene. Make sure the camera is on a steady surface, or fix it to a tripod (see pages 28-29). To make an exposure, push the lid all the way down. Pull the lid back up at the end of the exposure. You will need to experiment to find a good exposure time. Start by letting light into the camera for 15 seconds. Develop your print by following pages 36-37.

Try longer or shorter exposure times until the contrast on your final print is right. Reload your camera in a dark room for each exposure.

16 Focal Length

All cameras you buy today have a lens. When light enters a camera, all the light beams pass through the lens and change direction as we saw on page 7. Although light enters the camera from many angles, the image will focus at a single point inside the camera. The distance between the lens and this point is called the focal length of the lens.

You will need

card	glue
wire	scissors
a bradawl	thin dowel
a craft knife	thin balsa wood

1 With an adult's help, use a craft knife to cut a 16 cm x 5 cm balsa-wood base, with a central slit 1 cm short of each end.

MAKE it WORK!

This viewfinder shows you how lenses with different focal lengths give different **fields of view**, without moving nearer or further from the subject.

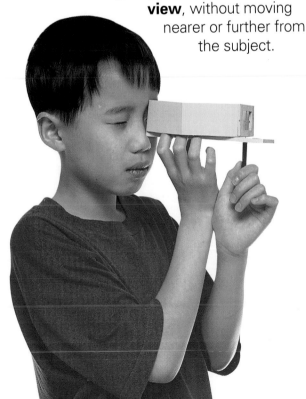

2 Cut two smaller pieces, both 5.5 cm long and 4.5 cm wide. Cut a window, 3.5 cm x 2.4 cm, inside each rectangle.

3 Glue one rectangle to the end of the base. Push stiff wire through the frame of the other rectangle to make a cross. The wire from top to bottom should be 7 cm long, so that it pokes through the slit in the base. Use a bradawl to make a hole in the end of a thin dowel. Push the wire into the dowel to make a handle.

4 With scissors, cut a 40 cm x 4.5 cm long strip of card with a hole in the centre. Position the hole over the fixed window. Now glue the card to the two windows and make folds as shown above.

5 Glue arrows to the base 3.8 cm, 5.8 cm, 8.5 cm and 13 cm from the fixed end of the base. These distances give the fields of view of the lenses on the opposite page.

Using your viewfinder

a **wide-angle** lens
with 18 mm focal length

35 mm lens

85 mm lens

105 mm
telephoto lens

Position the window at the arrow nearest to you. Look through the circle. The field of view, as shown right, is the same as a wide-angle lens, left.

Stand in the same position and move the window to the second arrow. You can now see the field of view of a 35 mm lens. This is similar to the view you can see through a standard camera.

Move the window to the third arrow. You can now see what it is like to look through an 85 mm lens.

With the window at the final arrow you will see how close an image can appear with a telephoto lens.

When you look through a special lens, called a fish-eye lens, you can see everything within a 180° angle. Fish-eye lenses were originally developed so that scientists could take photographs of the sky when studying astronomy or forecasting the weather.

Getting even closer

Macro lenses can produce images larger than your subject. Macro lenses are used for taking close-ups and magnifying objects up to 10 times.

A zoom lens is one that can change its focal length. If you have a camera with a zoom, you can take photographs over a range of fields of view without having to change lenses. Many small cameras have zooms.

1 With an adult's help, use a craft knife to cut the card, cardboard and plastic shapes shown. The black base should measure 20 cm x 15 cm x 10 cm. The red top box is 1 mm larger all round.

2 Cut a 2 cm diameter circle in the centre of the bottom flap of the card for the top box. Make a pinhole in the centre of the corresponding flap in the black card. Score along the dotted lines. Fold and glue the boxes using the tabs.

3 For your tripod attachment, cut a hole in the cardboard to fit the nut. Glue thin card over it to keep the nut in place and glue to the base box.

MAKE it WORK!
Pinhole cameras don't have lenses, but you can use a movable paper holder to see how different focal lengths give different fields of view.

You will need
photographic paper and a light-tight box
black corrugated plastic   thick cardboard
a nut with 1/4-in hole   a craft knife   a pin
two rubber bands   scissors   card

4 Line your base box with two sheets of corrugated plastic. The grooves act as slots in which you can position your paper holder.

5 To make the paper holder, place a piece of black card 15 cm x 10 cm on top of the card window. Fold the flaps up and tape them to the back of the card. You will need to load and unload your camera in a dark room as you did before. To make your prints, see pages 36-37.

▲ With the paper near the pinhole, a wider field of view is produced; the image appears smaller.

▲ When the paper is further from the pinhole, a smaller field of view is produced; the image appears larger.

Using your camera

Choose a scene to photograph and place the paper holder 10 cm from the pinhole. You have already found out the best exposure time for this length on pages 14-15. Make the exposure.

Unload the camera and keep your exposed paper in a light-tight box until you're ready to make your prints. Reload the camera and move the holder to a different position. When you increase the focal length make your exposures slightly longer. Make prints to see the results.

Draw lines on your camera to show the angle of view at each setting. Keep your empty camera together with rubber bands.

Most cameras use film rather than paper. Film is a thin strip of material coated with light-sensitive chemicals. The dull side of the film is the emulsion side. Cameras take different sizes of film because they have different formats. The format is the area of film exposed to light when you take a photograph.

Why film?

Using a camera which takes film rather than photographic paper has two advantages. As film is about 10 times more sensitive to light than photographic paper, you can take pictures using much shorter exposure times. This allows you to produce clearer shots, even when shooting moving objects. You can also enlarge and **crop** your image when you are making prints from film.

120 roll film

empty spool for 120

120 roll cameras

35 mm film

underwater disposable camera

old folding camera

compact camera

SLR camera

compact with zoom

Choosing a camera

All the cameras shown here are very common. Many of the older models can be bought cheaply from second-hand shops. You could use any of them, as well as the simple cameras that you can learn to make with this book, to practise photography.

Single lens reflex cameras (SLRs)

When you look through most cameras, the view through the viewfinder is slightly different from the view through the lens. But SLR cameras have a mirror system so that you see exactly what will appear on your photograph.

110 film

110 camera

a 35 mm colour negative

Formats
The format determines the shape of the final image. A 35 mm camera usually produces a rectangular view. The 120 and Polaroid cameras used here produce square views.

Before film was invented, photographers had to use pieces of glass coated with chemicals which needed to be processed immediately. This meant that photographers had to carry a huge amount of equipment with them.

Buying film
You can buy all of the film sizes on this page, but you may need to go to a photographic store to buy 120 films. Once you know the format you need, you have to decide whether to use black and white or colour film, and also whether to use negative or **transparency** film. You will also notice that films have different **ASA** numbers. A film with an ASA number of 200 is twice as sensitive to light as a film with an ASA of 100. With ASA 400 film you can take photographs indoors without a **flash**.

a 6 cm x 6 cm transparency produced by a 120 roll film camera

Polaroid film

Polaroid cameras
Polaroid cameras are very different from the other cameras shown here. They use special film which contains all the chemicals needed to process the image. A print is produced within minutes.

a Polaroid print

Polaroid cameras

22 Building a Camera

The shutter and aperture are parts of the camera that control the amount of light entering it. The aperture is an adjustable hole at the front of the camera. The shutter controls the length of time that the aperture is open to allow light to pass onto the film. You can change the size of the aperture and the speed of the shutter to let the right amount of light into your camera.

MAKE it WORK!

Over the following pages you will see how to make a simple camera which uses film. The first stage is to make a shutter. By making a shutter with a fixed speed you can see how shutters work.

You will need

thin brass available from model shops
0.5 cm thick balsa wood:
   one small block 2.5 cm x 1 cm
   one rectangle 12 cm x 7.5 cm
   two strips 12 cm x 1 cm
   two strips 6.5 cm x 1 cm
a compression hairspring
small pieces of matchstick
a selection of screws
black spray paint
tracing paper
a craft knife
a drill
glue

1 Trace these shapes to make your brass pieces. With an adult's help, drill small holes where the crosses are marked and spray the pieces black.

Dimensions: 75 mm (height), 120 mm (width), 35 mm, 30 mm, 45 mm, 8 mm, 25 mm, 45 mm

2 You will need to make holes and a slot on your balsa-wood rectangle as shown. The screw holes, marked as crosses, should only pass halfway through the board.

3 Glue balsa strips to the rectangle to make a shallow box. Paint the inside black. Place the keyhole-shaped piece of brass in position and screw it to the box. It should move from side to side. Fit two other screws to limit its movement.

4 Screw the crooked brass shape into place using two more screws. You need to bend the middle section of the shape so that the lower part stands away from the board.

5 Fit a long screw through the hole at the end of the crooked shape. Pass it through the slot to the top side of the box and into the small block of balsa wood. This is the shutter release button.

6 Glue two tiny pieces of matchstick and the hairspring to the brass pieces so that the hairspring is attached to the underside of the crooked piece and the top of the keyhole piece. Leave to dry overnight.

Looking at the shutter
To release your shutter, slide the button across. You will see the spring tighten. The lower brass piece will move quickly across the hole. To release again, move the button the other way and the brass will slide back across.

Changing shutter speeds
The shutter you have made has a fixed speed. Most cameras can change their shutter speed. Using a fast shutter speed you can freeze moving objects. With a slow speed you can deliberately blur images.

▶ This photograph of a disc spinning on a motor is taken with a slow shutter speed of 1/8 of a second.

▶ This photograph is taken with a medium shutter speed of 1/60 of a second.

▶ This photograph is taken with a fast shutter speed of 1/1000 of a second.

Making the body of your camera

Like the camera obscura and pinhole camera, a modern camera is a box that only lets light in when the aperture is open. Most cameras have a lens at the front which focuses light onto the film at the back. You can build onto your shutter to make a camera which takes pictures. Ask an adult to help you cut all of these pieces.

3 For the top, **c**, and the bottom, **d**, of the camera, cut two rectangles of 1.5 cm balsa wood, 12 cm x 3 cm. Make a 1 cm hole at one end of the top piece. At the other end make a hole the same size but only halfway through the wood. Do the same for the bottom piece. Paint the side with the half-made hole black for both the top and bottom.

You will need

balsa wood: 2 mm, 5 mm and 1.5 cm thick
a small brass cylinder 7 mm in diameter
strong double-sided tape
a nut with a ¼-in hole   a roll of film
an empty film canister   a craft knife
insulating tape   tape   a small lens
black paint   a saw   a paint brush

1 For the camera front, **a**, cut a 12 cm x 7.5 cm rectangle of 2 mm balsa wood. Cut a 2 cm hole in the centre. Paint it black.

2 For the camera sides, **b**, cut two rectangles of 5 mm balsa wood, 3 cm x 4.5 cm.

4 For the film frame, **e**, use four rectangles of 5 mm balsa wood to make a frame measuring 4.5 cm x 5 cm around the outside. The rectangles should be 1.8 cm wide. Cut a 4.5 cm x 5 cm piece of 2 mm balsa wood with a 3.5 cm x 2.4 cm central window. Glue this to the frame.

5 For the camera back, **f**, cut a 12 cm x 7.5 cm rectangle of 5 mm balsa wood. Cut a 4 cm square of 2 mm balsa wood and glue it to the centre of one side. Now paint this side black.

6 For the winder, **g**, saw two slots in the end of the cylinder so that it clips into the end of a film canister. Glue this to a piece of balsa wood.

7 Open the empty canister and tape the end of your film to the inner part, as shown above. Close up the canister.

8 Finish your front section by gluing **a** to the open side of the shutter mechanism you made on pages 22-23.

9 Glue the sides to the bottom and glue the frame to the top. The hole in the top is diagonally opposite the hole in the bottom.

10 Place your film in the middle section. Slot the frame in front of the film and stick the top to the sides with double-sided tape.

11 Stick the back, middle and front sections together with insulating tape. Make a frame for your lens with small pieces of thin balsa wood .

12 Stick the lens to the front of your camera with double-sided tape. Tape over all joins and slot the winder in place.

Ready to go!
Glue the nut to the bottom or side of your camera so that you can put it on a tripod and tape over the hole at the bottom of your camera. You are now ready to take photos.

Between each shot, you will need to wind the key through about one-and-a-half turns. When you have finished your film, take your camera into a dark room. In red light, take off the tape covering the bottom hole and use the key to wind the film back into the original canister. You will need to undo the tape to unload and reload your camera.

The aperture is the hole which the shutter uncovers when you take a picture. On many camera lenses, the size of the aperture is changed using a ring marked with numbers called f-stops. As the f-stop numbers get lower (from f 5.6 to f 4, for example) the aperture gets larger, letting more light into the camera.

MAKE it WORK!

The camera you made on pages 24-25 has an aperture which cannot change size. With a little extra work you can convert this camera so that it has an aperture with three different settings. You will need to remove the lens from your camera before you start.

You will need
thin brass sheet
a craft knife
stiff wire
scissors
a drill
glue

1 With scissors, cut three brass strips, 1.5 cm x 7.5 cm. With an adult's help, make three holes in one of the pieces 3 mm, 6 mm and 10 mm wide.

2 Glue the two blank strips of brass on either side of the hole, leaving enough space for the strip with holes.

3 Position the centre strip of brass as shown, so that it can slide up and down. Bend the ends of the brass strip away from the camera.

4 Fix the lens and frame back on to the camera, gluing the balsa wood to the two outer brass strips. The centre strip should move freely. Bend the wire to form a viewfinder and attach this to the front of the camera with tape.

Varying your aperture

On page 23, we saw why you might want to let less light into the camera by using a quicker shutter speed. When would you want to let less light into the camera using the aperture? Using a standard 35 mm camera you can see the effects of adjusting the aperture.

You will need

a camera with a variable aperture and shutter
coloured card numbers as below
stiff wire   Plasticine

123456

1 Fix the numbers on wire and stick each one into Plasticine. Position the numbers at different distances in front of your camera. Make sure all six numbers are in view.

2 Take photographs at different f-stops. You should focus on the nearest number each time. As you make the aperture smaller, you will need to use a slower shutter speed so that enough light enters the camera. If you are taking the pictures indoors, you may need to use a flash.

▶ With a large aperture, only the numbers nearest the camera are in focus. As the aperture gets smaller, more numbers appear in focus. With the smallest aperture, all the numbers are in focus. We can see that a small aperture gives a greater **depth of field**.

Using the aperture and shutter together

If you make the aperture bigger by one setting, the amount of light entering the camera doubles. If you make the shutter speed faster by one setting, the amount of light entering the camera halves. To photograph a moving scene without blurring your image, it is best to use a fast shutter speed and a large aperture. For a shot that needs a good depth of field, use a small aperture and a slower shutter speed.

The muscles in your eye work in a very similar way to the aperture in an automatic camera. Your pupil is a hole which lets light into your eye. When you walk into a dark room, the muscles in your eye make your pupil larger. This lets more light into your eye. When you look at a bright light, your pupil gets smaller.

▲ f 1.8

▲ f 2.8

▲ f 5.6

▲ f 22

Tripods are
very useful.
They hold cameras steady so you
can take photographs that need long
exposures. At night, for example, you
need to allow more time to let light
into the camera. A tripod also supports
your camera if you want to take a series
of photographs from the same position.

MAKE it WORK!

Make a simple tripod for your pinhole camera,
or any camera that has a ¼-in threaded hole.
Ask an adult to help you cut and drill the pieces.

You will need

blockboard	cardboard tube
three bolts with wing nuts	a hacksaw
a wooden dowel 70 cm long	screws
a headless bolt and a 1 cm nut	a drill

nine 2.5 cm x 1 cm wood strips:
   three 65 cm long, six 70 cm long
two small and three large jubilee clips
three rubber washers and six metal washers

1 With a hacksaw, round off one end of the
six 70 cm strips. Drill a hole in each, 0.5 cm
from the rounded end. Cut a blockboard triangle
with 12 cm sides. Drill a 2.5 cm central hole and
six smaller holes, as shown left.

2 Cut three 4 cm x 2 cm blockboard rectangles,
drilling a hole, off centre, in each. Place a
rectangle on its side so the hole is nearer to you
than to the triangle. Screw the pieces together.

3 Sandwich the rectangle of wood between
two of the round-ended strips and secure with
a studding screw, washers and a wing nut.

4 Drill a 1 cm hole 2 cm from one end of the
dowel. Drill a hole through the centre of the
dowel big enough for the screw. Push the nut
into the hole and screw in the headless screw.

5 Push the dowel through the hole in the centre of the triangle. Add two pieces of cardboard tube, 4 cm long, one either side of the triangle. Move the dowel to the height that you want and fix it in place by tightening the two small jubilee clips either side of the tubes.

6 Slot a 65 cm wooden strip in the middle of each tripod leg. Fix in place with a large jubilee clip at the bottom. Now you can vary the height of the tripod by moving the centre wood strips up or down and tightening the jubilee clips.

7 Complete your tripod by screwing rubber washers to the bottom of each foot.

Using a tripod
Fix a camera to your tripod and try a simple **time-lapse photography** experiment. Ask a friend to blow up a balloon. Take a shot every couple of seconds to make a sequence as the balloon gets bigger. The tripod keeps your camera in position so that the photo frame does not change. You can make a zoetrope, as on pages 44-45, to **animate** the sequence.

By taking photographs of a plant at regular intervals during a day, botanists study how plants move and grow. They put these photographs together to make a film and see how plants move to follow the Sun.

30 Lighting a Shot

When you are taking pictures outside, you can change the look of your photograph by standing with the Sun behind you, in front of you or to the side. You can light objects indoors in the same way to give different effects.

MAKE it WORK!

As you move a lamp around a collection of objects indoors, the changing shadows make the objects appear very different. Take photographs of your scenes using a tripod.

▲ back lighting: objects are lit from behind with the light pointing up from the floor

You will need
two double bulldog clips
black and white card
a desk lamp
Plasticine
gels

1 Cut the card to make the cone. Tape it together and fasten it to the lamp with Plasticine. Ask an adult to check that your bulb is not too strong as this could cause the paper to get hot and even to burn.

2 Card flaps give a wide band of light. To use them, take the cone off the lamp and fix two large squares of black card to your lamp with the clips.

▲ side lighting: objects are lit from the left using the card flaps

3 Make several boxes from the card and model some shapes from Plasticine as below.

Setting your scene

Place the objects on a table 1 m from a wall. Light them using the cone to give a spotlight effect and the card flaps to give a wide band of light. Change the appearance of the scene by lighting it from different angles.

▲ front lighting: objects are lit from the front using the card flaps

Looking at colour
Investigate the effect of colour by putting coloured gels in between the objects and your light source. Place a transparency in front of your light source to create an effect like the one shown at the bottom of this page.

▲ side lighting: objects are lit from the right using the card flaps

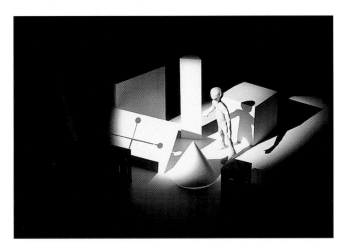

▲ spot lighting: objects are lit from the front using the card cone

When a film is exposed to light, chemical changes take place on the emulsion side. These changes form an imprint of the scene you have photographed. The image is invisible at this stage so you need to process your film with chemicals in a light–tight tank so you can see the image.

Making your tank

1 Fold the rubber bands in half and loop them through the bulldog clips. Attach the rubber bands to the cork bungs with the staples.

2 With an adult's help, drill a 1.5 cm hole near each end of the drainpipe.

MAKE it WORK!

Make a processing tank to hold film and prepare your solutions: developer, fixer and water, ready to process your own black and white film.

To prepare your tank and solutions you will need

two rubber bands`	glue
two rubber bungs	a jug
two fence staples	a drill
two large cork bungs	a saw
75 cm plastic drainpipe	a hammer
film processing solutions	rubber gloves
three measuring cylinders	a thermometer
two small balsa-wood strips	two bulldog clips

3 To make a 'light trap', ask an adult to help you saw a short piece of drainpipe in half lengthways. Glue the balsa-wood strips inside one end of the tank on either side of the hole. Glue the underside of these strips and slide in, and press on, the piece of drainpipe.

Making up solutions

You need to dilute developer and fixer solutions before use. This means that you need to mix a small amount of each one with water. Ask an adult to help you prepare them.

Be careful!

You can make up your solutions in the light in an ordinary room, but take care not to splash them over you. Always wear rubber gloves and keep a window open nearby.

1 You will need to make about 500 ml of each solution. If, for example, the dilution is 1:9 for the developer, pour 50 ml of developer into the measuring cylinder.

2 Use a thermometer to check the temperature of the water. It should be a little warmer than recommended on the bottle so that when it is mixed with the cold developer, the solution will be the right temperature.

3 Add water to the developer. If the recommended dilution is 1:9, for example, add 450 ml to the 50 ml of developer. Now prepare your fixer solution to the recommended dilution. Then fill your third cylinder with water.

film spiral

winder

tank

film canister

light-tight lids

Processing tanks

You can buy processing tanks which are more sophisticated than the one you have made. The tanks are light-tight and, once the film is inside, and the top is in place, the chemicals can be poured into and out of the tank through the lid in normal room light.

MAKE it WORK!

Having made your tank and completed a roll of film, you can now go into a dark room and process your film. You can follow the steps shown below if you are using a commercial tank too, but you will need to follow the manufacturer's instructions to load the film into the tank. Remember to take regular breaks outside the dark room and to wear rubber gloves when you are pouring the solutions.

developer   water   fixer

You will need

your solutions: developer, fixer and water

a jug	a timer	scissors
a funnel	a dark room	
plastic tubing	rubber gloves	
a jubilee clip	a completed film	
a sink or bucket	your processing tank	

What do the solutions do?

The developer changes the chemicals in the image area to produce an image you can see. After developing, you put the print in water to stop the image developing any more. The fixer makes the developed image permanent.

Processing a film

1 Arrange the equipment so that you can find the objects in the dark. It is a good idea to practise loading the tank in the light using an old piece of film.

2 Turn off the light and force open the top of your film roll using a coin. Cut off the narrow part of the film and attach the end to one of the bulldog clips.

3 Ease the film into the pipe. Push the cork into the end and let the film spool fall through to the other end of the pipe.

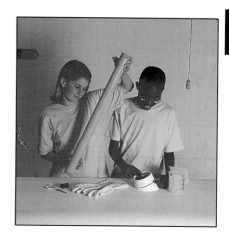

4 Cut the film at the other end of the pipe. Attach this end of the film to a bulldog clip in the same way as for the top. Push the cork into the end of the pipe.

5 Put a rubber bung in the hole that does not have the light trap in place and turn on the safety light. Use a funnel to pour about 500 ml of developer into the other hole.

6 Put a bung in this hole. Set the timer as recommended on your developer bottle. Rock the drainpipe to make sure that all parts of the film are covered by the solution.

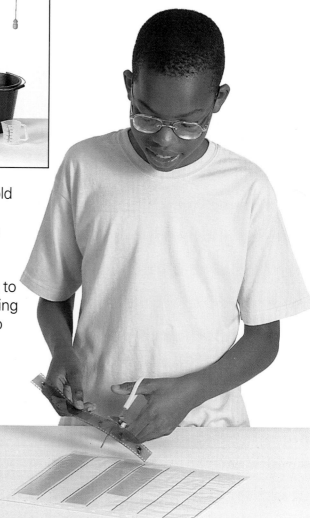

7 At the end of the developing time, remove the bung from one end and carefully empty the solution into a sink or bucket. Repeat 5, 6 and 7 using water instead of the developing solution. Repeat 5, 6 and 7 once more for the fixer solution. You can now switch the light on.

8 Fix the tubing to a cold tap with a jubilee clip and pour water into the drainpipe to rinse the film. This takes about 10 minutes, so it's best to have your water emptying into a sink. If there is no sink nearby, empty the bucket as it fills up.

▶ To dry your film you can attach one end to a washing line using a bulldog clip. Put another clip at the other end of the film so it doesn't curl up. When the film is dry, cut your negatives into strips and store them until you are ready to make prints.

The image on a piece of exposed photographic paper, such as the paper in a pinhole camera, is invisible. You need to develop the paper, as with film, in order to see the picture you have taken. A machine called an enlarger is used to shine light through negatives onto your paper to make prints.

MAKE it WORK!

In a dark room, develop your own pinhole camera prints. Then use the negative prints to make positive images. You will need to use different solutions from those used to process a film.

You will need

a watch	a sink or bucket
rubber gloves	three plastic trays
a plastic funnel	a measuring cylinder
a thermometer	two pairs of plastic tongs
photographic solutions for developing prints	

Making up solutions

Ask an adult to help you dilute your solutions as on page 33. Fill your trays, 1 cm deep, with your solutions: put developer in the first tray, water in the second and fixer in the third. Before you start developing your print, read from the bottles how long you will need to leave the paper in each tray.

Developing prints

1 Turn the safety light on. With gloves on, slide the paper into the developing tray for the recommended time.

2 Gently rock the tray so that the paper is covered evenly and kept moving in the liquid while developing.

3 When the time is up, remove the paper with tongs and drop it into the water for a few seconds. Rock as before.

4 Now slide the paper into the fixer tray for the recommended time and rock the tray.

5 Remove the print from the fixing solution and turn the room lights on.

6 Rinse the print in water in a sink or a bucket. Peg your print to a line and let it dry.

Making a positive print

positive print

negative print

1 With the safety light on, put the fresh photographic paper, emulsion side up, on your surface.

2 Place the negative print, shiny side down, on top of the paper and cover with the glass to keep the sheets flat.

Your pinhole camera print

The developed print from your pinhole camera will be a negative image. You can use this negative to make a positive **contact print**. You will need some scissors, fresh photographic paper, photographic solutions, a torch and a piece of glass taped along its edges for safety. Again, you will need to do your work in a dark room.

3 Shine a bright torch through the glass for five seconds. Develop the positive print in the same way as you developed the first print. If the image is not dark enough, try again with a longer exposure time.

Before taking the trouble to enlarge and print a negative you need to find the one that contains the best image. Contact strips are small positive prints made by placing negatives on photographic paper and shining light through them. From the contact strip you can choose the best image and then go on to make an enlarged print.

MAKE it WORK!

You can take some shots of a Plasticine figure, changing the settings of either the aperture or the shutter speed. Then you can make a contact strip showing the same image at different light exposures.

You will need

photographic paper and a light-tight box
a camera with a variable aperture and
  shutter speed
a black and white film for your camera
a piece of glass with taped edges
a dark room
a tripod

1 First take a series of photographs of your object. Use a tripod to keep your camera steady. Keep either the shutter speed or aperture constant and take eight photographs, changing the other setting each time. Write down the settings as you go.

2 After processing, take your film into the dark room. Turn the safety light on and place a sheet of photographic paper, shiny side up, on a clean surface.

3 Place the negatives, emulsion side down, onto the paper and cover with the sheet of glass.

best exposure

best exposure

Many small cameras have been invented for use in surgery and espionage but the smallest commercial camera is the round Japanese 'Petal' camera. It has a diameter of 2.9 cm and a thickness of 1.65 cm. The largest and most expensive camera ever built is the 27-tonne Rolls Royce camera built in 1956. It is 2.69 m wide and 14.02 m long.

4 Turn the light on so that you expose the paper for a few seconds. Switch back to red light and put the paper into a light-tight box.

5 Develop your contact strips using the technique used on pages 36-37.

Looking at your contact strip

Choose the best image from the contact strip and use the corresponding negative to make your print using an enlarger. Note the aperture and shutter settings used to produce the right exposure so you can use the setting next time.

◀ On your negatives, the under-exposed shots are quite light. The negatives are darker where the shots have been exposed to more light.

◀ You can see the same effect on the contact strip, but, because these are positive images, the lights and darks are reversed.

◀ Transparency film gives a positive image. From a positive image you can identify the best exposure without making a contact strip. To view a transparency, light is projected through it so that a large image is made on a screen.

The enlarger is a piece of equipment for making prints from film negatives. Light shines through the negative and projects a larger image on to a piece of photographic paper. With an enlarger you can make different-sized prints from the same negative. You can also improve your print by controlling the amount of light reaching some areas of the paper.

MAKE it WORK!

You can choose one of the negatives from which you made a contact strip on pages 38-39 and enlarge it to give prints of different sizes. Enlargers are expensive machines so you may need to join a photography club so you can use all the right equipment.

You will need

photographic paper and a light-tight box
scissors   a dark room
negatives   a contact frame
an enlarger   a watch or timer

lamp

height adjuster

lens

negative carrier

contact frame

1 In the safety light, put the negative strip in the carrier so that the image you want to enlarge is centred in the frame.

2 Turn on the enlarger and adjust the height until the image on the contact frame is the size you want.

3 Now turn the focusing knob until the image on the contact frame is sharp. Now turn off the enlarger.

4 Take a sheet of photographic paper from its box. Position the paper on the contact frame so that the metal arms of the frame keep the paper in place.

5 Make a test strip, as below, to find the best exposure time. Turn the enlarger and timer on. When the time is up, put your paper in a box ready to develop.

Dodging
You can lighten parts of a print by moving a dodger over a dark area for some of the exposure time. The dodger stops light reaching this area. Make a dodger by fixing a circle of black card to stiff wire with tape. To darken areas, you need to make a hole in a piece of black card. After exposing the paper once, make a second exposure with the card in place so that only the area needing extra light is exposed.

a dodger

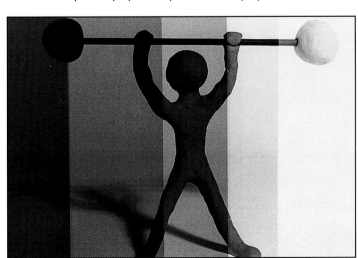

25 seconds   5 seconds

Making a test strip
You should make a test strip to find the ideal exposure time. To do this, use a piece of black card to expose a narrow strip for five seconds. Move the card back every five seconds to expose four or five further strips until all the paper is uncovered. When you develop the paper you will be able to see which exposure time gives the best contrast.

Photograms are pictures made without a camera. They are made when objects are placed on photographic paper which is then exposed to light. The objects stop light from reaching parts of the paper. So, when the paper is developed, an image of the objects is produced. You can use all sorts of everyday objects to create different effects.

MAKE it WORK!
Make photograms like the ones on these pages using photographic paper and some small objects.

You will need
photographic paper and a light-tight black box
small objects e.g. clips, pins, pens, toys
a dark room and safety light
a torch

1 Turn the safety light on and lay out a piece of photographic paper shiny side up. Place your chosen objects on the paper and then shine a torch light on the paper from above for about 10 seconds. If you are using flat objects you could make a test strip to find the ideal exposure time for your print, as shown on page 41. Be careful not to move the objects.

2 When you have finished exposing, put the paper in your black box until you are ready to develop your prints.

3 Follow the developing process described on pages 36-37.

The first photograms were made in the middle of the 19th century. In Britain, Anna Atkins, thought to be the first woman photographer, made a beautiful handmade book of prints using this process. She used different types of seaweed to make blue negative prints, called cyanotypes.

Experimenting with photograms

When you have made some photograms with opaque objects, try using objects which let some light through, such as pasta or flower petals, or transparent objects, such as a glass bowl or some spectacles. Try shining the torch at an angle through a wine glass. You can make double exposures by exposing the paper twice, using different objects each time.

Drawing with light

If you place a cone of card over the end of your torch, you can use the beam of light that comes through as a 'light pen'. Draw several lines on different parts of the paper by turning the torch off, moving it and then turning it on again. The prints shown above have been made in this way.

Using different grades of paper

Try making the same photogram on different grades of paper. The difference between paper grades lies in the number of shades of grey between white and black, they can produce. A soft paper (grade 1) produces an image with lots of shades of grey. A hard paper (grade 5) gives the least number of tones and produces an image in black and white, with very few shades of grey.

In the 19th century, before the invention of cinema, people had toys called zoetropes. A zoetrope is a cylinder with slits which has pictures on the inside. When you spin the zoetrope around and look through the slits, it appears as if the pictures are moving.

1 Cut a strip of black card the same length as your 13 prints placed next to each other. Cut another strip a little longer and twice as wide. Cut 13 slits equally-spaced, as shown. The slits should be 5 mm wide.

MAKE it WORK!
You can make a zoetrope by making a cylinder and lining it with 13 contact prints that you have taken and developed yourself.

You will need
a sequence of small prints
scissors and a craft knife
black and yellow card
a plastic plant pot
a pin

2 Glue the ends of the wide strip together to form a cylinder. You can put yellow card over the bottom of the black cylinder to give it extra support. Cut a circular base the same size as the cylinder and tape it in place.

▲ Using wire and Plasticine, you can make a figure to photograph.

3 Push a pin through the centre of the base and into the bottom of an upturned plant pot.

4 Glue your series of prints along the narrow strip and glue this along the bottom edge of the inside of your cylinder.

Moving pictures

Sit on the floor and spin the cylinder.
Look at the pictures through the slits. As the zoetrope moves around, the images should appear to move. You will need to experiment with the speed of your zoetrope to see what speed gives the best effect.

How do zoetropes work?

When you see a sequence of pictures at the rate of more than 13 frames per second, your brain puts the images together and you think you are seeing a moving scene. In films and videos the images appear to move much more smoothly because 24 frames are shown every second.

The word 'zoetrope' comes from the Greek meaning 'wheel of life'.

Animate To make separate pictures appear as if images are moving.

ASA ASA stands for the American Standards Association. It is a system of numbers used to describe the sensitivity of a film to light.

Concave lens A lens which bends light so that the beams of light travel away from each other.

Contact prints Prints made by shining light through a negative which is lying flat on a piece of photographic paper. A contact print is always the same size as its negative.

Contrast The difference between the dark and light areas on prints and negatives, i.e. how grey it is. An image with high contrast has clear areas of light and dark. An image with low contrast has a wider range of greys between light and dark areas.

Convex lens A lens which bends light so that the beams of light meet at a point.

Crop To block out parts of an image that you don't want to print.

Depth of field In a photograph, the distance between the nearest point that is in focus and the furthest point that is also in focus is called the depth of field. If you take a photograph of two objects at different distances from you, both images are more likely to appear in focus if you use a small aperture.

Develop To use chemicals to see an image on photographic paper or film which has been exposed to light.

Dilute To make a liquid weaker by adding water to it.

Energy When something has energy it has the ability to make things move, change or warm up. Torches and lamps change electricity into light energy which can be detected by our eyes.

Expose To allow light to fall on photographic film or paper. In a camera an exposure is made when the shutter is open.

Field of view The field of view is how much you can see when you look through a camera. Different lenses e.g. telephoto and wide angle, give you different fields of view.

Flash A device which produces a burst of light. It is used to make a dark scene brighter so that it can be recorded on film.

Focus To move a lens so that the image it produces is as clear and sharp as possible.

Gel A thin coloured sheet of plastic which allows light of its own colour to pass through, but which blocks out light of other colours.

Image A picture of something.

Inverted Turned upside down. An inverted image is one that appears upside down.

Lens A specially-made piece of glass which can bend light.

Negative An image in which light and dark areas are reversed. The black areas appear white and white areas appear black. Developed film is often called a 'negative'.

Opaque An object which is opaque does not allow light to pass through it. Wood, for example, is opaque.

Over-exposed Reached by too much light. An over-exposed photograph is one taken with an exposure that lets too much light into the camera. Your printed positive image will be too pale and some parts of the scene may not appear at all.

Positive An image which has shades of black and white and colour that are the same as that of the object.

Print An image that is recorded on photographic paper.

Reflect To bounce light back. We see objects because light beams reflect off them.

Refract To bend light. Some objects such as lenses, or jars of water, allow light to pass through them but cause the light to change direction.

Telephoto lens A lens which makes objects seem to be much nearer than they really are. It has a long focal length and a narrow field of view.

Time-lapse photography Photographs taken at different times and then put together to make a film. The effect is to show events which take place very slowly over hours or even days, in just a few seconds.

Transparency A type of film that gives a positive image.

Transparent An object which is transparent allows light to pass through it.

Under-exposed Not reached by enough light. An under-exposed photograph is one taken with an exposure that doesn't allow enough light into the camera. Your printed positive image will be very dark.

Wide-angle lens A lens which has a wide field of view.